JUSTIN BIEBER

100% UNAUTHORIZED

WRITTEN BY SUE McMILLAN

EDITED BY PHILIPPA WINGATE,
DESIGNED BY ZOE BRADLEY,
COVER BY ANGIE ALLISON

BARRON'S

PLANET JUSTIN

At the tender age of 18, Justin Bieber has achieved more than most people will manage in a lifetime. It's hard to believe that his whirlwind rise to fame began when he was just 12 years old. When the Biebs uploaded videos of himself singing to YouTube, it was the start of his roller-coaster ride from small-town boy to international megastar.

BIEBER FEVER

It took just a few months for Justin to rack up an amazing ten million hits online—Bieber Fever had truly begun! Scooter Braun, an executive director at So So Def Recordings, spotted Justin's awesome talent and quickly signed him to Island Records.

In no time, Justin became a chart-topping sensation. Soon he was jetting around the world to perform for his millions of adoring fans—known as Beliebers—who all wished Justin was their "Boyfriend."

BELIEVE

Three hit albums later, the Biebs has an unbelievably hectic schedule, packed with red-carpet appearances, VIP parties, and award ceremonies. Add to that the sell-out tours, recording sessions, and photoshoots, and you will realize that Justin is a very busy boy!

SUCH A TWEET BOY

Despite his hectic schedule, JB still finds the time to keep in touch with his fans. He tweets over 22 million followers with regular updates about his albums and tours—on April 18, 2012, he tweeted: "just finished cutting one of the most important records of my life. an amazing and strange feeling at the same time. #HONORED."

JB will never forget that he owes everything to his fans and tweeted: "MY RELATIONSHIP with MY BELIEBERS = EVERYTHING."

ACCESS ALL AREAS

This book is your backstage pass to the secret world of the hottest singer on the planet. It's packed with news and gorgeous pictures of the star everyone's talking about.

So what are you waiting for?

It's time to explore Planet Bieber ...

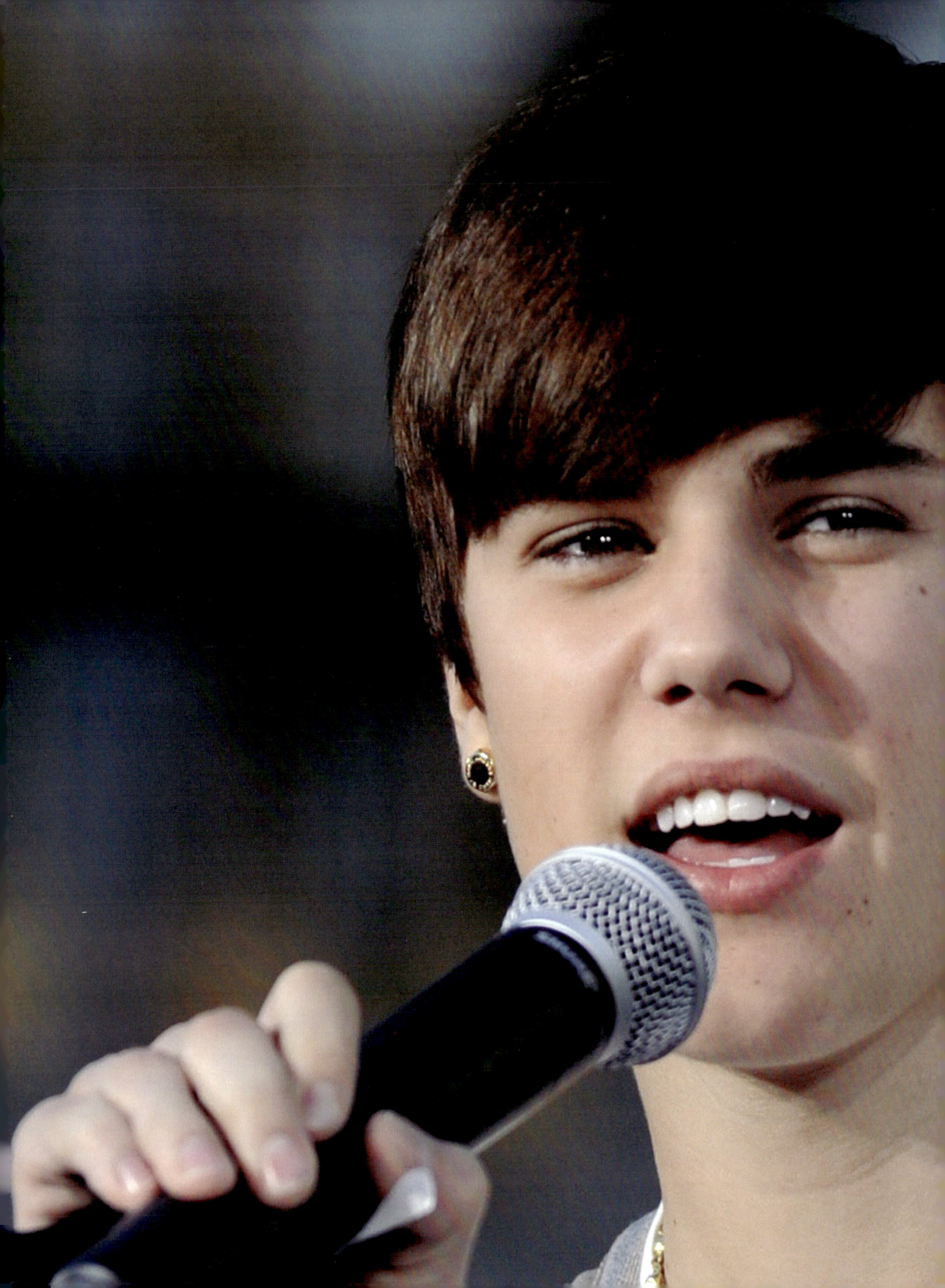

THE BIEBER FILES

BIEBER BASICS

FULL NAME:	Justin Drew Bieber
NICKNAMES:	J-Biebs, JB, the Biebs
DATE OF BIRTH:	March 1, 1994
HAIR & EYES:	Brown
NATIONALITY:	Canadian
HOME TOWN:	Stratford, Ontario, Canada
LIVES:	Atlanta, Georgia, USA
PETS:	Sam, a papillon dog

FIRM FAVORITES

LIKES:	Apple pie
REALLY LIKES:	Girls
COLOR:	Purple
FOODS:	Spaghetti bolognaise, cheesecake, and Swedish Fish candy
DRINK:	Orange juice
MUSIC VIDEO:	"Thriller" by Michael Jackson
TV SHOW:	*Smallville*
HASHTAGS:	#Believe, #Beliebers, #Ilovemyfans
IDOL:	Wayne Gretzky, a former ice hockey player
CELEB CRUSH:	Beyoncé

PET PEEVES

DISLIKES:	When girls try to impress him, being asked his favorite color, being cold, getting up early in the morning

INSIDE INFO

CELEB BUDDIES:	Usher, Taylor Swift, Drake, Jaden Smith, Lil Wayne, Sean Kingston, Chris Brown, One Direction, and The Wanted
DREAM JOB:	Architect
HIDDEN TALENTS:	Can solve a Rubik's cube in under a minute
LEFTY OR RIGHTY?:	Left-handed
PLAYS:	Drums, guitar, trumpet, and keyboard
PIERCINGS:	Both ears, wears studs
TATTOOS:	A bird on his left hip, the word "Jesus" in Hebrew on his ribs, and a pic of Jesus and praying hands on his lower leg
SUPER-POWER WISH:	To fly

TRUE OR FALSE?

Are you Justin's number one fan? Find out with these tricky teasers—all you have to do is decide if the following statements are true or false. The answers are on page 24.

1. When he was 16, Justin's dad took him to get a tattoo.

2. When Justin had his hair cut off in February 2011, a clipping was auctioned for charity.

3. Justin loves big, round sunglasses on girls.

4. Justin's first tweet was on September 17, 2009.

5. The Biebster really wants to meet President Obama.

6. JB starred in two episodes of the TV series *CSI*.

7. JB has his own line of nail polishes and perfume.

8. Justin has a Bart Simpson pendant made out of diamonds and sapphires.

9. The Biebster's two best friends are named Rodney and Charlie.

10. The Biebs was "slimed" at the 2012 Nickelodeon Kids' Choice Awards.

JUSTIN IN NUMBERS

If you love Justin 100%, you might be interested in some other numbers that are all about the Biebs:

• Justin has more than 22 million followers on Twitter.

• The Biebs gets about 60 new mentions on Twitter every second.

• Despite being a popstar, Justin had to keep up with his education and had an impressive grade-point average of 4.0, so he was a straight-A student—A for Adorable that is!

• In April 2012, during a trip to London to promote his album, *Believe*, the phone-lines in Justin's hotel were jammed by more than 12,000 Beliebers, all desperate to speak to their idol.

• His favorite number is 6.

• Justin recently said, "Well, by 25 or 26, I want to see myself, like, married or start looking for a family."

• On its release in April 2012, "Boyfriend" hurtled straight into the top ten in the Billboard Chart in the U.S., with more than half a million copies downloaded in one week. And in the U.K., "Boyfriend" sold an impressive 54,817 copies in its first week.

• JB makes a brief appearance on the big screen as an alien in *Men in Black 3*.

• The Biebs stands at a yummy 67 inches (170 cm) tall—that's 5 feet and 7 inches of JB.

• Naughty Justin once tweeted someone else's phone number, pretending it was his. The real owner received 26,000 text messages!

ALL AROUND THE WORLD

All around the world, Beliebers are crazy for Justin. Here's a handful of the crazy things that have happened on his tours.

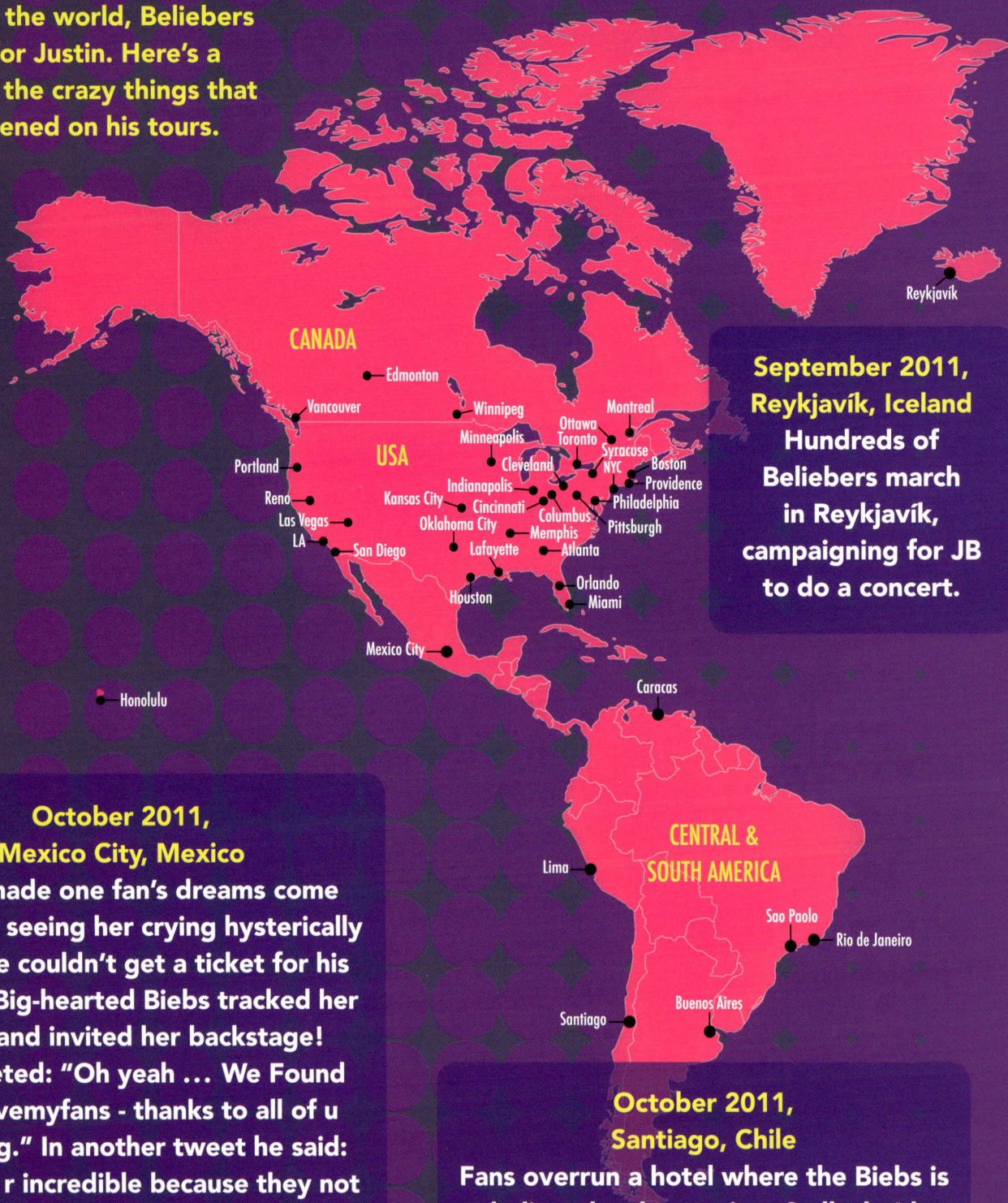

CANADA

Edmonton
Vancouver
Winnipeg
Montreal
Portland
Minneapolis
Ottawa
Toronto
Syracuse
NYC
Boston
USA
Cleveland
Providence
Reno
Indianapolis
Philadelphia
Las Vegas
Kansas City
Cincinnati
Columbus
Pittsburgh
LA
Oklahoma City
Memphis
San Diego
Lafayette
Atlanta
Orlando
Houston
Miami

Mexico City

Honolulu

Reykjavík

Caracas

Lima

CENTRAL & SOUTH AMERICA

Sao Paolo
Rio de Janeiro

Santiago
Buenos Aires

September 2011, Reykjavík, Iceland
Hundreds of Beliebers march in Reykjavík, campaigning for JB to do a concert.

October 2011, Mexico City, Mexico
Justin made one fan's dreams come true after seeing her crying hysterically when she couldn't get a ticket for his concert. Big-hearted Biebs tracked her down and invited her backstage! He tweeted: "Oh yeah ... We Found Her. ilovemyfans - thanks to all of u 4 helping." In another tweet he said: "My fans r incredible because they not only care for me but each other."

October 2011, Santiago, Chile
Fans overrun a hotel where the Biebs is believed to be staying. Sadly, he'd stayed an extra day in Argentina. The star was asked to fly in by helicopter, to avoid being mobbed by the girls.

April 2012, London, U.K.
Thousands of Beliebers gather at The Royal Garden Hotel, Kensington. They all have one thing on their mind—to see their idol. Two fans faint when he flashes his chest at the window. JB tweets: "eating a steak and gonna get a good night's rest and relax. I hear u guys outside the hotel and I LOVE U!"

April 2011, Milan, Italy
Justin tweets: "love italy. best food ever! show was incredible and the party was fun. thanks for the good times. Now off to the Israel! #myworldtour"

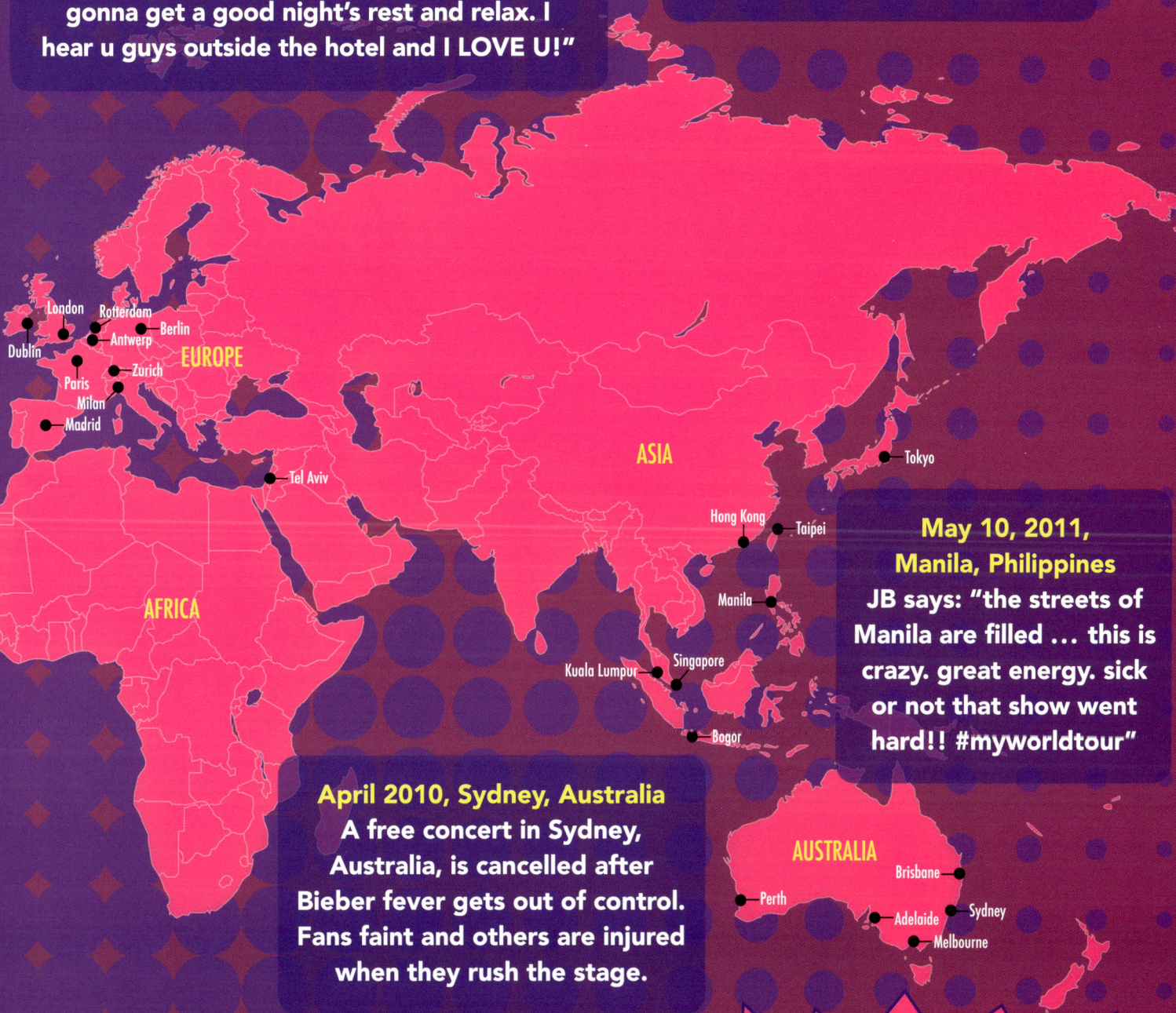

London
Rotterdam
Berlin
Dublin
Antwerp
Zurich
EUROPE
Paris
Milan
Madrid

Tel Aviv

ASIA

Tokyo

Hong Kong
Taipei

Manila

AFRICA

Kuala Lumpur
Singapore

Bogor

May 10, 2011, Manila, Philippines
JB says: "the streets of Manila are filled ... this is crazy. great energy. sick or not that show went hard!! #myworldtour"

April 2010, Sydney, Australia
A free concert in Sydney, Australia, is cancelled after Bieber fever gets out of control. Fans faint and others are injured when they rush the stage.

AUSTRALIA
Brisbane
Perth
Adelaide
Sydney
Melbourne

AND COMING UP ...
Who knows what the Believe Tour will hold, but the last word goes to the man himself: "planning trips for ALL AROUND THE WORLD for #BELIEVE – see u all soon! I LOVE U. THANKS."

BIEBER STYLE

Geek-chic, over-sized shades, and high tops remain a key part of the Bieber look, but over the years Justin has matured from baseball-cap-wearing kid to edgy trend-setter ...

EARLY DAYS

Bursting onto the scene in 2009, the Biebs was all about baseball caps and tees. His cute, laid-back style was an immediate hit with his fans. They went crazy for his luscious locks, and his trademark style was copied by boys around the world.

The big shocker was the day he CUT HIS HAIR! February 21, 2011 is a day no true fan will ever forget. The hot news spread rapidly, and Beliebers were divided over the loss of his floppy swoop which was replaced by a new, choppier style.

HOTTIE!

Since "haircut day," the Biebs has sported all kinds of hairstyles, from slick and spiky to a retro quiff. As he has matured, Justin's choice of clothes has become more confident, with fitted, streamlined pieces. He's a guy who's comfortable with his look whatever he's wearing. His relaxed style means he's equally happy in a sharp suit or in jeans and a hoodie. One thing's for sure—Justin knows how to rock a look.

TREND TIMELINE

2009
MARCH 28: At the Nickelodeon Kids' Choice Awards, a baggy tee, jeans, and trademark high tops are part of the star-in-the-making's look.

SEPTEMBER: Justin's look develops. Brighter colors, dog tags, and a crucifix are added to his wardrobe.

2010
MARCH: First inking—a bird on his left hip.

Justin gets daring with geek-chic glasses and takes fashion risks as he wears bright jeans and statement pieces like a furry hunter hat.

Justin wears slick rock-star threads and an edgy leather jacket.

2011

JANUARY 16: The Biebs rocks a sophisticated look in a cool suit for the Golden Globes.

FEBRUARY 21: Chops his lovely locks.

FEBRUARY 27: Justin and Selena Gomez wow the crowds at the Vanity Fair Oscars Party. Gorgeous in a black velvet tux, he even adds a bright red hanky to match Selena's stunning red dress.

APRIL: Tattoo—this time the word "Jesus" in Hebrew is inked vertically on his left side over his ribs.

MAY: The Biebster sports a tattoo of a star on his elbow. Not long after it's gone—turns out it's a henna tattoo!

JUNE: The Biebs gets pierced. Appears at the MTV Movie Awards with cool studs in both ears.

2012

JANUARY 6: Sports a new Jesus tattoo on the calf of his left leg.

JANUARY 16: Justin rocks a new, darker hair color.

JANUARY 28: Attends the NRJ Music Awards in Cannes, France, in a bright jacket with slicked-back hair.

MARCH: Justin gets inked again—this time he has an image of praying hands added to his left leg.

APRIL: His hair is teased into a quiff as he films the video for "Boyfriend."

KEY PIECES TO ROCK THE LOOK

- All things purple
- Dog tags
- Hoodie
- Geeky over-sized specs
- High top sneakers
- Stud earrings

ANSWERS

TRUE OR FALSE? (PAGE 12)

1. True. Justin got his first tattoo, a bird, on his hip. He's since added more, including the word "Jesus" in Hebrew on his side, and a tattoo of Jesus and praying hands on his lower leg.

2. True. A single lock of Justin's hair raised an impressive $40,668 for an animal rights charity.

3. False. Justin told *Seventeen* magazine that he thinks the big, round sunglasses look is "kind of over-rated."

4. False. His first tweet was on May 11, 2009. It said: "Check out my single 'ONE TIME' on my myspace and spread the word for me. Thanks."

5. False. The Biebs has met President Obama twice. First back in 2009, and he also sang a Christmas carol at an event in December 2011.

6. True. He starred in two episodes as a troubled teen called Jason McCann.

7. True. Justin's range of nail polishes, the "One Less Lonely Girl" line, sold out when they were launched in 2010. His perfume, "Someday," hit the shelves in June 2011.

8. False. He has a diamond and ruby pendant, worth a cool $25,000, of *Family Guy*'s Stewie Griffin.

9. False. Their names are Ryan and Chaz.

10. True. Justin was covered from head to toe in green gunk.

PICTURE ACKNOWLEDGEMENTS

Front cover: Jason LaVeris/FilmMagic/Getty Images
Back cover: George Pimentel/WireImage/Getty Images
Large poster: Action Press/Rex Features

Page 1: Matt Boster/SIPA/Rex Features; pages 2: Startraks Photo/Rex Features; page 3: Startraks Photo/Rex Features; page 5: Dimitrios Kambouris/Rex Features; pages 6-7: Stewart Cook/Rex Features; page 8: Brian Rasic/Rex Features; page 10: George Pimentel/WireImage/Getty Images; page 11: Pascal Le Segretain/Getty Images; page 13: Brian Rasic/Rex Features; page 14: Picture Perfect/Rex Features; page 18: David Fisher/Rex Features; page 19: Matt Sayles/AP/Press Association Images; pages 22–23: George Pimentel/WireImage/Getty Images; page 24: Ethan Miller/Getty Images. background graphics: ShutterStock Inc.

First edition for North America published in 2012 by Barron's Educational Series, Inc.

First published in Great Britain in 2012 by Buster Books, an imprint of Michael O'Mara Books Limited, 9 Lion Yard, Tremadoc Road, London SW4 7NQ www.mombooks.com/busterbooks

Copyright © Buster Books 2012

All inquiries should be addressed to:
Barron's Educational Series, Inc.
250 Wireless Boulevard
Hauppauge, NY 11788
www.barronseduc.com

PLEASE NOTE: This book is not affiliated with or endorsed by Justin Bieber or any of his publishers or licensees.

ISBN-13: 978-1-4380-0211-8

Library of Congress Control No.: 2012941193

Date of Manufacture: July 2012
Manufactured by: V05I05N, Shenzen, China

Printed in China